Birds

Anita Ganeri

Watts Books
London • New York • Sydney

© 1994 Watts Books

Watts Books
96 Leonard Street
London EC2A 4RH

Franklin Watts Australia
14 Mars Road
Lane Cove
NSW 2066

UK ISBN: 0 7496 1589 3

10 9 8 7 6 5 4 3 2 1

Dewey Decimal Classification 598.2

Series editor: Pippa Pollard
Editor: Jane Walker
Design: Visual Image
Artwork: Mike Atkinson
Cover artwork: Mainline Design
Photo research: Alison Renwick
Fact checking: Simone K. Lefolii

A CIP catalogue record for this book
is available from the British Library

Printed in Italy by
G. Canale & C. SpA

Contents

What are birds?

Birds are not difficult to find. You only have to look up into the sky. But what makes a bird? There are many ways of telling birds apart from other animals. All birds have beaks, wings and feathers. Most birds can fly, though not all. Many have **hollow** bones to make them lighter in the air. All birds lay eggs, often in nests.

▽ Colourful macaws live in the Brazilian rainforest. Can you see all their bird features?

All kinds of birds

There are about 9,000 different kinds of bird. They all share some of the same features but there is a wide range of bird sizes, shapes and colours. There are tiny hummingbirds, huge ostriches, long-legged flamingos, soaring albatrosses and many, many more. Birds are divided into almost 30 groups. The biggest group is the perching birds, such as sparrows and crows.

▷ Ducks and geese belong to a group of waterbirds. They live in lakes, ponds and rivers.

▽ The Andean condor is a bird of prey. It soars over the mountains on its huge wings.

4

Ostrich

▷ The ostrich is the biggest of all birds. It is taller than a tall person. It cannot fly but it can run very fast.

▷ The bee hummingbird is the smallest bird. It is only as big as a butterfly.

Bee hummingbird

Where do birds live?

Birds live all over the world, on land and near water. Many live in towns and cities. Birds can travel far and wide because they are able to fly. They are also **warm-blooded**, like mammals. This means they can stay warm and active even if the weather is cold. Many birds have special features to help them survive in different parts of the world.

▷ Emperor penguins live in the icy Antarctic. They have extra-thick feathers for warmth.

▷ Toucans live in the rainforests of South America. They use their huge bills for reaching and cutting fruit.

▽ In the desert, a male sandgrouse works hard finding water for his chicks. He soaks his breast feathers in water for the chicks to drink.

◁ The jacana has very long feet and toes for walking over water lily leaves without sinking.

Fine feathers

Birds are the only animals with feathers. Feathers are light and strong. They are made from the same material which makes your fingernails and hair. A bird has different feathers for different jobs, as you can see opposite. Birds **preen** their feathers with their beaks to keep them clean and tidy. Once or twice a year, their old feathers fall off and they grow a whole new set.

▷ Fluffy down feathers keep birds warm.

▷ Short body feathers give birds their shape.

▽ Birds bathe in dust or water to clean their feathers.

▽ Long stiff wing and tail feathers help birds to fly and steer in the air.

▽ Male peacocks spread their tail feathers out in a fan to impress females.

Flying

Birds are not the only animals that can fly. Bats and insects can fly too. But birds are the best fliers of all. Their bodies are light and **streamlined**, making them perfect for flying. Birds have different ways of flying. Some flap their wings, using very strong chest muscles. Others soar or glide, or even hover.

▷ Hummingbirds beat their wings so fast that they can hover in one place.

▽ The peregrine is the fastest bird. It can dive through the air at a speed of 180 kilometres per hour.

▷ The wandering albatross has long, slender wings for gliding. It can soar for days on end over the ocean.

10

Long-distance travellers

Some birds make long journeys every autumn. They fly to warmer places where they spend the winter. They return home in spring. This journey is called **migration**. Some birds fly thousands of kilometres, without getting lost. They seem to use the Sun, stars and Moon to find their way. They also use mountains and rivers as signposts.

▷ Crowds of swallows gather on trees and telephone wires, ready to fly off for the winter.

▽ Each year, the Arctic tern flies from the Arctic all the way to the Antarctic and back.

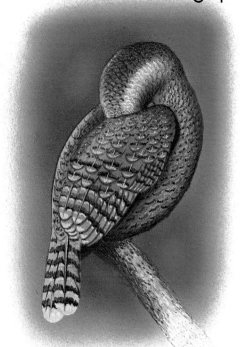

△ The poorwill does not migrate. Instead it spends the cold winter months in a deep sleep.

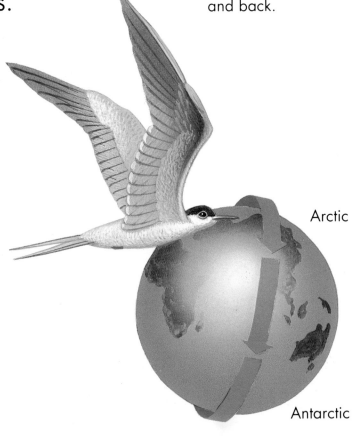

Arctic

Antarctic

12

▽ Barnacle geese migrate in huge, V-shaped flocks. They take it in turns to lead the flock.

What do birds eat?

Birds need lots of **energy** for flying, so they have to eat plenty of food. Birds eat many different things. They eat seeds, plants, worms, **nectar**, fish and insects. Some birds eat one type of food only. Birds of prey, for example, are meat-eaters. Birds do not have teeth so they cannot chew their food. Some swallow grit and stones to help them grind up food in their stomach.

▷ As their name suggests, flycatchers eat flies and other insects.

▽ Flamingos tip their huge bills upside down in the water to sieve shrimps and tiny plants and animals. They get their pink colour from the food they eat.

▷ Vultures feed on
the bodies of dead
animals. They pick
the bones clean.

◁ A heron waits by
the water's edge.
When a fish swims
by, the heron grasps
it with its sharp beak.

Bills and beaks

Birds catch their food in their beaks or **bills**. The size and shape of a bird's beak depend on what that bird eats. Finches, for example, have short, strong beaks for eating seeds. Birds of prey have sharp, hooked beaks for tearing meat. Hummingbirds have long, thin bills for reaching deep into flowers to suck up the sweet nectar.

▷ A pelican has a huge stretchy pouch under its bill for scooping up fish.

▽ A crossbill has a criss-crossed bill. It is perfect for getting seeds out of pine cones.

▽ The oystercatcher uses its long bill to dig for shellfish and open them up.

Finding a mate

Birds have to find a **mate** so that the female can lay eggs which hatch into baby birds. Male birds often compete for the females. They have many ways of getting their attention. Some males show off their bright feathers. Others sing or dance. Some bring the females gifts of food or put on flying displays.

▷ Male birds of paradise show off their beautiful feathers to win over a mate.

▽ A male frigate bird blows up the pouch of skin on its throat like a big red balloon.

◁ The satin bowerbird builds an arch of twigs to attract a female mate. It decorates the arch with blue objects such as berries and feathers.

18

Building a nest

Many birds build nests as warm, safe places to lay their eggs and bring up their babies. They use materials such as plants, twigs, leaves and mud to build their nests. They line them with soft moss, feathers or wool. There are many different sizes and shapes of nests, from tiny cups to huge platforms high up in the trees.

▷ Ovenbirds build big domed nests of mud and grass.

◁ Eagles build huge, heavy platforms of branches as their nests. They use the same nests year after year.

▷ Lots of sociable weaver birds build their nests in the same tree.

△ The hermit hummingbird's tiny nest is held together with cobwebs.

Hatching out

A female bird may lay just one egg a year, or as many as ten eggs at a time. Some eggs have coloured shells to hide them from enemies. One of the parents sits on the eggs until they hatch. This keeps them warm so that the baby birds grow properly. Some chicks leave the nest as soon as they hatch. Others have to be fed by their parents until they are able to fly away.

▷ Plovers lay their eggs on the beach. The eggs and the baby birds look like small pebbles.

▽ The ostrich lays the biggest eggs. One ostrich egg is about the size of 20 chicken's eggs.

△ A kingfisher lays its eggs at the end of a riverbank tunnel. The parents bring fish to feed the baby birds.

Birds in song

Birds sing and call to each other. This is their way of talking to each other. Some birds sing to win over a mate and to warn other birds to stay away from their nests. Birds also chirp and tweet to keep in touch with each other, for example when they are migrating. The most famous talking birds are parrots and mynah birds.

▷ When kept as pets, parrots can often copy what people say to them.

△ Nightingales sing their musical songs at night.

◁ Male snipes do not sing but they shake their tail feathers to talk to their mate.

▽ The cuckoo is named after the sound of its call.

25

Bird senses

Most birds have good hearing and good eyesight. Many can see much better than people can. The best eyes belong to the birds of prey. They hover high in the air, then swoop down on their prey with great accuracy. Some birds are **nocturnal**. They use their **senses** to find food and their way around in the dark.

▷ A golden eagle has superb eyesight for spotting hares and rabbits on the ground far below.

▽ The kiwi uses its sense of smell to find insects and worms at night. Most birds cannot smell very well.

▷ Owls have excellent hearing and eyesight for hunting their prey at night.

Birds in danger

When people cut down forests, or **pollute** rivers and seas, many birds lose their wild homes. If they cannot survive in other places, they die out (become **extinct**). Today, more than 1,000 types of bird are at risk of becoming extinct. Some are losing their homes. Others are shot for food or for sport. Some of the rarest birds are being caught and sold as pets.

▷ Kakapos are very rare, flightless parrots which live in New Zealand. Only about 50 of these birds are now left.

▽ There were once only 30 Bali starlings left in the world. More starlings have now been bred in zoos and released back into the wild.

△ The dusky seaside
sparrow became
extinct as recently
as 1987.

▷ Dodos once lived
on the island of
Mauritius. Sailors
discovered them in
the 1500s. Less than
200 years later, the
dodos had all been
hunted and killed.

Things to do

If you are interested in birds and would like to know more about them, there are lots of places you can write to for information. Here are a few useful addresses:

RSPB (Royal Society for the Protection of Birds)
The Lodge
SANDY
Bedfordshire
SG19 2DL

This society studies and helps to protect all sorts of British birds. It runs a Young Ornithologists Club especially for young members.

The British Trust for Ornithology
The National Centre for Ornithology
The Nunnery
Nunnery Place
THETFORD
Norfolk
IP24 2PU

This society organises field trips to watch and study birds.

World Wide Fund for Nature (WWF)
Panda House
Weyside Park
GODALMING
Surrey
GU7 1XR

The WWF is trying to save endangered animals, including birds, all over the world.

Watch
c/o The Royal Society for Nature Conservation (RSNC)
22 The Green
Nettleham
LINCOLN
LN2 2NR

A conservation group especially for young people.

Glossary

bill Another word for a bird's beak.

energy The ability to go, to move and to do work. Birds get their energy from the food they eat.

extinct No longer exists on Earth. An animal which has died out is said to be extinct. For example, the dodo is a well-known extinct bird.

hollow Something which is not solid but has a hole or empty space inside it. Birds have hollow bones which are very light to make flying easier.

mate Male and female birds find a mate so that the female can lay eggs. The eggs will hatch into baby birds.

migration A journey, often a long one, which many birds make each autumn. They fly off to spend the winter in warmer places and return in spring.

nectar A sweet, syrupy liquid that is made deep inside flowers.

nocturnal Active at night. Nocturnal birds, such as owls, hunt for food at night. They rest during the day.

pollute To make dirty or spoil.

preen To keep clean and tidy. Birds preen their feathers with their beaks.

senses The ways that animals have of finding out about the world around them. The five senses are smell, sight, taste, touch and hearing.

streamlined Having a smooth shape to move easily through air or water.

warm-blooded Able to keep warm without relying on the weather. A warm-blooded animal, such as a bird, can keep its body temperature about the same no matter how hot or cold it is outside.

Index

Photographic credits:
Bruce Coleman Ltd (H Reinhard) 25;
NHPA (B Beehler) 19, (S Dalton) 11,
27, (N Dennis) 9, 14, (B Hawkes)
21, (E Pott) 17, (K Schafer) 7, (P Scott)
13, (Silvestris Fotoservice) 4,
(M Strange) 28, (R Tidman) 23,
(M Wendler) 3.